Kitchen
Witchen

A note from the author

It has become evident to me, that today the human species is either reconnecting with or awaking to, what seems to be an intimate connection to mother Earth. I see it in our daily living as vegan and plant-based diets become more common. I've taken notice of the rise in meditation practice and holistic medicines amongst my generation. Mostly I've witnessed the amazing numbers of people who are looking into themselves and outward into the universe for answers in life rather than religion. The large population who are now looking to their ancestors for guidance and to the elements of Earth for assistance. It's an evolution that is happening so fast to so many. Transitioning into a new way of life, thinking and living requires a level of support and understanding. Magical Beginnings started to be just that. As a way for me to assist those new to, struggling or simply growing in their journey. A community forum where we can openly discuss these so called "taboo" issues such as magic, spells (energy harnessing and manipulation) deities and God self. A safe place where we can learn and grow together and make the absolute best out of this physical and temporary experience called life. Still in its infancy, Magical Beginnings has developed into so much more. Still answering questions directly via social media, I am now blessed with the time to share knowledge through video discussions on my YouTube channel. As well as to now be able to provide products and services to aid on your spiritual journey via my online shop. It is a privilege to be of assistance to others and to witness the growth of our spices. The knowledge and experiences I occur and absorb will always be at your disposal.

Much Ase' and Namaste

Disclaimer

The information presented in this book is a
collection of research gathered from Pagan,
Hoodoo and Chinese spiritual systems myths,
lore and beliefs. The author makes no claims
to any supernatural power of any ingredients
listed. The information in this book is presented
as curious and for informational purposes only.
The author does not encourage the use or
incorporation of these ingredients in any spell,
ritual or practices mentioned inside this book,
or otherwise nor do I assume any liabilities for
the uses of. Further, this book is not intended
as a substitute for medical advice from a
physician. The health benefits listed should not
be considered as medical advice. The author is
not a medical doctor and does not encourage
the use of any ingredient listed as a form of
medical treatment, nor do I assume any liability
for the uses of these ingredients as medical
treatment. The reader should regularly consult
a physician in matters regarding his/ her
health. In respect to symptoms that require
emergency or immediate medical attention the
reader is advised to call 911

Preface

If someone were to ask me "which is the most magical room in my home?" hands down my response would be the kitchen. Personally, I harness more energy within my kitchen walls than in any other room of my apartment. Conversing with my higher self while doing dishes, being mindful of the direction in which I stir my pots, enchanting ingredients, giving thanks for my food before it's consumed. Most magical of them all, is the amount of love and care that goes into preparing a meal for the ones I love the most. These are daily actions that allow me to invoke, amplify and apply powerful, positive emotions and energies to my everyday magic and spiritual practices. And then of course there's the ingredients. No matter if your intent is healing, hexing, love or prosperity, from the cupboard to the fridge the kitchen has got you covered. Magical Beginnings "Kitchen Witchen" is a collection of common kitchen and supermarket found ingredients that you can incorporate into your everyday magical and spiritual practices. No matter what your niche, candle magic, tinctures and tonics, spiritual baths or creating charms and talisman. Designed to complement any beginner or advanced practitioner. This book is a treasure trove of knowledge and information that will serve you for years to come.

How to use this book

Every ingredient listed in this book is accompanied with seven subcategories: Energy type, Element type, Planetary/ Deity associations, Magical correspondences, Common magical uses, Health benefits and a witchy tip or lore. Below is a breakdown of each subcategory and its purpose. These examples are only the beginning of what all can be done with the knowledge presented in any specific subcategory. This is provided only to inspire the reader in the many ways each is useful.

Energy- Know the energy type of the ingredient you have chosen to use.
If you're conjuring a love spell and your target is male, incorporating ingredients with both a masculie energy type as well as love correspondence, would sync the desired energies better than one who's energy type was femine and love corresponding.

Element- Acknowledge the elements associated with your choice of ingredients. into your
If your casting calls ingredients who are mostly associated with the element of fire, you might consider using candles or some other element

of fire to complement.

Planetary/ Deity associations- Utilize the connection.
Planetary associations are a great tool for timing spells and ritual. Casting using specific ingredients while its commanding planet is in alignment, a specific phase, retrograde etc. allows for an energetic connection, empowering your magical working. It's the same concept with deity associations. If you conduct a spell or ritual under the guidance or protection of a specific deity, incorporating ingredients or leaving an offering of an ingredient favored by said deity may help them to show favoritism your way.

Magical Correspondences- It's all about intent
Use this section to identify the magical properties of a specific ingredient.

Magical Uses- Get inspired
This section lists common magical uses for ingredients.

Health Benefits- See disclaimer

***Witchy tip/ Lore**- From witch to another
Tips, tricks and lore on every ingredient listed, from my own personal book of spells as well as from sister and brother witches who have

passed down their practices from generations.

Magical Beginnings

Kitchen Witchen

A part of the 'Everyday Magic" Series

Written By
Ebony S. Jefferson

Almonds

Energy-Female/ Yin
Elements- Air, Fire
Planetary/ Deity Associations- Jupiter, Mercury/
Chandra, Cybele, Ptah, Thot, many of the Greek
Gods/Goddesses
Magical Correspondences: Beauty, Devotion,
Fertility, Love, Prosperity, Success, Self sufficiency,
Wisdom
Magical Uses: Carrier oil, Talisman
Health Benefits: High in fiber and vitamin E, assist
in lowering blood sugar and cholesterol, headache
relief, boost energy

Lore* Carry a almond inside of your pocket to help
you locate items lost

All Spice

Energy- Masculin/ Yang
Elements- Fire
Planetary/ Deity Association- Sun, Mars
Magical Correspondence: Courage, Healing, Luck,
Male fertility, Money, Positivity, Strength
Magical Uses: Incense, Talisman
Health Benefits: Possessing antioxidant,
anti-inflammatory, cancer-fighting, sedative,
antiseptic, antiviral and antifungal properties. Aides
in digestion and reduces flatulence

Witchy tip * Wrap allspice in green cloth and carry on you to attract and maintain prosperity

Apple

Energy- Femine/ Yin
Elements- Air
Planetary/ Deity Association- Venus/ Bes, Idun, Hera
Magical Correspondences: Beauty, Fertility, Friendship, Happiness, Healing, Immortality, Knowledge, Love, Temptation
Magical Uses: Talisman
Health Benefits: High in fiber and vitamin C, promotes healthy teeth and bones, regulates blood sugar, lowers risk of cancers, liver detox, helps prevent alzheimer's disease

Lore* Slice an apple in half and share with your lover to evoke happiness into the relationship

Avocado

Energy- Female/ Yin
Elements- Water
Planetary/ Deity Associations- Venus/ Elegba, Osiris, Thot
Magical Correspondences: Beauty, Love, Lust, Power
Magical Uses: Carrier oil, Talisman

Health Benefits: High in vitamins C,E,K, B6, copper and magnesium. Biotin rich, promotes healthy skin, hair and nails.

Witchy trip* Plant an avocado seed inside or in front of the home to attract love

Anise Star

Energy- Masculine/ Yang
Elements- Air
Planetary/ Deity Association- Moon, Jupiter/ Apollo
Magical Correspondence:Astral Travel, Awareness, Divination, Fertility, Love, Lust, Prevents nightmares, Protection, Return a lover, Spiritual energy
Magical Uses: Incense, Talisman
Health Benefits: Antioxidant, antifungal, antibacterial properties, relieves cold and flu symptoms in infants, helps with milk production in nursing mothers, aides symptoms of depression

Witchy tip* Burn star anise during divination or dream work for clearer visions

Baking Soda

Energy- Femine/ Yin
Elements- Air
Planetary/ Deity Associations- Earth

Magical Correspondences: Aura boosting, Banishing, Cleansing, Protecting, Removes unwanted energy
Magical Uses: Powder, Spiritual Bath
Health Benefits: Natural antacid, relieves symptoms of UTI and gout

Witchy tip* Keep a box of baking soda near when doing fire rituals/ burnings incase of emergencies where the fire gets out of hand

Banana

Energy- Femine/ Yin
Elements-Water
Planetary/ Deity Associations- Venus
Magical Correspondences: Abundance, Fertility, Focus, Love, Good luck, Prosperity, Success
Magical Uses: Powder
Health Benefits: High in magnesium and potassium, boost energy, good for eye and bone health

Lore* Eating a banana after meditation/ spirit quest is said help you retain the information received

Blackberries

Energy- Femine/ Yin
Elements- Water, Air
Planetary/ Deity Associations- Earth, Venus/ Bridget,

Magical Correspondences: Female fertility, Healing, Love, Money, Protection
Magical Uses: Amulet, Powder
Health Benefits: Anti Inflammatory, Anti aging, improves cardiovascular health

Witchy tip* Use blackberry thorns mojo bags for protection

Basil

Energy- Masculine/ Yang
Elements- Fire
Planetary/ Deity Association- Mars/ Krishna, Vishnu, Ezrulie
Magical Correspondence: Business, Divination (love matters),Fertility, Fidelity, Happiness, Influence, Love, Money, Peace, Psychic protection and development Success
Magical Uses: Incense, Candle dress
Health Benefits: An excellent source of vitamin K, manganese, iron, vitamin A, and vitamin C. Antibiotic, antifungal, reduces anxiety and headache pain, Supports liver function and supports a healthy gut.

Witchy tip* Add basil to bathwater to remove bad luck associated with finances

Bay leaves

Energy- Masculine/ Yang

Elements-Fire
Planetary/ Deity Associations- The Sun
Magical Correspondence: Banishment,
Consecration, Divination, Empowerment, Exorcism,
Fidelity, Healing, Loyalty, Psychic development,
Spell breaking, Success,Transformation, Wishes,
Winter rituals
Magical Uses: Talisman
Health Benefits: A rich source of vitamin A, vitamin
C, iron, potassium, calcium, and magnesium.
Reduces anxiety, relieves chest colds and arthritis,
regulates menstrual cycle.

Lore* Write wishes, hopes and dreams onto a
bayleaf and burn under a full moon to make come
true

Black Pepper

Energy- Masculine/ Yang
Elements-Fire
Planetary/ Deity Associations- Mars
Magical Correspondents: Banishing, Binding, Stops
gossip, Wards of jealousy, Protection, Exorcism,
Confusion, Commanding, Hex breaking, Curses
Magical Uses: Talisman
Health Benefits: High antioxidant properties, with
benefits against bacterial growth, particularly in the
intestinal tract. Aides in digestion, helps fight cold
and flues, increase nutrition absorption, clears
sinus.

Witchy tip* Add black pepper to freezer jar spells to keep target away

Carrot

Energy- Masculinie/ Yang
Elements- Fire
Planetary/ Deity Associations- Earth, Mars
Magical Correspondences: Fertility, Lust, Dispel Illusions, Grounding
Magical Uses: Potion
Health Benefits: High in vitamin K and A, regulates blood sugar, boost immune system

Cashew

Energy- Masculine/ Yang
Elements- Fire
Planetary/ Deity Associations- Sun
Magical correspondences: Increase income, Money
Magical Uses: Powder
Health Benefits: Contains vitamins E and B6, promotes healthy bones, skin and hair, inhibits the growth of gallstones

Witchy tip* Ground cashew shells and add to prosperity powders and spells

Cayenne

Energy- Masculine/ Yang
Elements- Fire
Planetary/ Deity Associations- Mars

Magical Correspondence: Banishment, Empowerment, Heartbreak, Hot footing, Increase spiritual strength, Protection, Romance, Separation, Speeds spells
Magical Uses: Candle dress, Talisman
Health Benefits: High in vitamin A and E, boost metabolism, aids in digestion, relieves pain.

Witchy Tip* Dress a red candle with cayenne and rose bud, burn to add strength to spells of passion

Celery

Energy- Masculine/ Yin
Elements- Fire, Water
Planetary/ Deity Associations- Mercury
Magical Correspondences: Dream magic, Fertility, Increase mental powers, Lust, Passion, Psychic strength
Magical Uses: Powder, Talisman
Health Benefits: Good source of folate, potassium and fiber. Supports heart health, lowers blood pressure, relieves symptoms of UTI and gout

Cherries

Energy- Femine/ Yin
Elements- Water, Air
Planetary/ Deity Associations- Venus
Magical correspondence: Divination, Fertility, Love attraction, Substitutes blood in spells
Magical Uses: Charms, Amulets, Potions
Health Benefits: Anti- Inflammatory , Diuretic, Promotes healthy eyesight, increases appetite

Witchy tip* Add two cherry pits into an amulet to

increase male fertility.

Chilly Powder

Energy- Masculine/ Yang
Elements- Fire
Planetary/ Deity Associations- Mars
Magical correspondence: Banishment, Boost
spells, Fertility, Hex breaking, Love, Lust,
Passion, Prevents unwanted guest, Protection
Magical Uses: Charm
Health Benefits: Prevents acid reflux, antioxidant,
helps reduce fat, kills ulcer causing bacteria in the
gut.

Witchy tip* Sprinkle chili powder onto floors then
sweep up to prevent unwanted guest

Cinnamon

Energy- Masculine/ Yang
Elements- Air, Fire
Planetary/ Deity Associations- Sun, Venus/
Aphrodite, Bast
Magical Correspondence: Attraction, Clairvoyance,
Cleansing, Divination, Fast money, Good luck,
Healing, Love, Passion, Prosperity, Protection, Sex
magic, Spirt walks
Magical Uses: Incense, Talisman
Health Benefits: Anti inflammatory with antidiabetic
properties, Lowers blood sugar, reduces stress,
relieves car sickness, reduce the risk of heart
disease

Lore* Tie 3 cinnamon stick together with green string, hang over door of business to attract customers

Cloves

Energy- Masculine/ Yang
Elements- Fire
Planetary / Deity Associations- Jupiter / any Malaysain Deity
Magical correspondents: Attraction, Clairvoyance, Compelling, Divination, Love, Memory, Passion, Prosperity, Protection, Purification, Stops gossip, Wealth
Magical Uses: Inscensce, Charm, Tonic
Health Benefits:High in antioxidants, Reduces inflammation, Aphrodisiac, Promotes bone growth, Kills bacteria, Relieves tooth pain

Witchy Tip* Steep cloves in boiling water, add salt and lemongrass for oral pain relieving tonic

Coconut

Energy- Femine/ Yin
Elements- Water
Planetary/ Deity Associations- Moon/ Obatala, Isis, Athena, Asar, Aset, Osiris
Magical Correspondences: Chastity, Confidence, Enhanced sexual attraction, Protection, Purification
Magical Uses: Charm, Talisman, Spiritual Bath
Health Benefits: Rich in fiber, immune boosting. Promotes healthy teeth and gums

Lore* Hang whole coconuts over the doorway of
your home to keep out harm

Coffee

Energy- Masculine/ Yin
Elements- Fire, Earth, Air
Planetary/ Deity Associations- Mars, Mercury,
Uranus/ Archangel Gabriel, Chango
Magical Correspondences: End nightmares,
Focus, Happiness, Luck, Lust, Offering to deities,
Removes blockage, Romance,Speeds spell results,
Spell booster
Magical Uses: Incense, Floor wash, Spiritual bath
Health Benefits: Increases energy and focus, boost
mood, Diuretic effect may help relieve symptoms of
gout and UTI, may improve liver dysfunctions like
cirrhosis and cancer

Witchy tip* Drink black coffee before spell work and
meditation to improve focus

Corn

Energy- Femine/ Neutral
Elements- Earth, Fire
Planetary/ Deity Associations- Sun, Venus/
Xochipilli
Magical Correspondences: Divination, Fertility,
Immortality, Longevity, Luck,
Protection
Magical Uses: Incense, Talisman
Health Benefits: Contains Vitamin B12, Folic acid
and iron, Boost energy, promotes health skin

Lore* Burn red corn husk during labor to quicken

the delivery

Crushed red peppers
Energy- Masculine/ Yang
Elements- Fire
Planetary/ Deity Associations- Mars
Magical Correspondences: Banishment, Fidelity,
Hex removal, Hot footing, Keep away unwanted
guest, Love, Overcome a broken heart, Passion,
Seperation, Spiritual strength,
Magical Uses: Talisman
Health Benefits: High in vitamins C, B6, antioxidant,
aides in digestion, boost metabolism, relieves
migraines

Witchy tip* Mix crushed red peppers with charcoal
and devil's shoestring, place in the path of an
enemy to keep them far away

Cucumber
Energy- Femine/ Yin
Elements- Water
Planetary/ Deity Associations- Moon/ Uttu
Magical Correspondences: Chastity, Fertility,
Ending lustful behavior, Healing
Magical Uses: Inscensce, Talisman
Health Benefits: Low in calories high in nutrients,
promotes hydration and regulation of bowels, great
for skin

Cumin
Energy- Masculine/ Yang
Elements- Fire
Planetary/ Deity Associations- Mars/ Venus
Magical Correspondents: Defense, Empowerment,

Exorcism, Fidelity, Hex breaking, Lust, Passion,
Politics, Protection
Magical Uses: Inscensces, Talisman
Health Benefits: Aphrodisiac, high in iron, promotes
digestion, eases colic, stops diarrhea

Lore* It said that adding cumin and lavender into
your bedding will ensure fidelity from your partner

Curry Powder

Energy- Masculine/ Yang
Elements- Fire
Planetary/ Deity Associations- Mars
Magical Correspondence: Keeps away evil,
Protection
Magical Uses: Charm
Healing Benefits: Anti inflammatory, anti aging,
aides in liver detox, boost metabolism, promotes
healthy bones.

Witchy Tip* Burn curry powder to invoke blessings
of protection

Dill Weed

Energy- Masculine/ Yang
Elements- Fire
Planetary/ Deity Associations- Moon, Mercury
Magical Correspondence: Blessings, Confidence,
Determination, Friendship, Keep secrets,Protection,
Luck, Lust, Mental clarity, Money, Romance,
Peace, Psychic protection
Magical Uses: Charm

Health Benefits: A good source of fiber, calcium and folate. Reduces gas and bloating.

Witchy tip* Anoint a green candle with dill weed, cinnamon and basil, burn for fast money

Eggs

Energy- Femine/ Yin
Elements- Water
Planetary/ Deity Association- Moon/ Ishtar, Phanas
Magical Correspondences: Chaos, Cleansing, Divination, Fertility, Healing,Hexing,Protection
Magical Uses: Powder, Talisman
Health Benefits: High in amino acids, promets healthy hair and nails, increase good cholesterol levels

Lore* Crack a room temperature egg into water when in heavy doubt. If the yolk floats your ans is yes/ positive if it sinks the answer is no/ negative

Fennel Seeds

Energy- Masculine/ Yang
Elements- Air, Fire
Planetary/ Deity Associations- Mercury, Neptune/ Prometheus, Dionysus
Magical Correspondence: Commanding, Consecration, Divination, Diet spells, Focus, Healing, Love, Memory, Midsummer rituals, Protection of home and body, Purification
Magical Uses: Charm
Health Benefits: Anti inflammatory,

Antifungal,Antibacterial, lowers blood pressure, reduces acne, boosts metabolism

Witchy tip* Carry fennel seeds to prevent spiritual attack

Garlic

Energy- Masculine/ Yang
Elements- Fire
Planetary/ Deity Associations- Mars, Saturn / Cybele, Hecate
Magical Correspondence: Adds strength to other spell ingredients, Breaks spells, Courage, Divination, Exorcism, Healing, Longevity, Lust, Money, Passion, Prevents nightmares, Protection, Protects against thieves, Psychic protection, Removes negative energy, Stops gossip
Magical Uses: Charm, Talisman, Tonic
Health Benefits: Improves libito, Treats ear infection, cold sores and athlete's foot, Reduces the risk of colon/ prostate cancers

Witchy tip* Make protection powder for floors, windows and doorways by mixing garlic powder and egg shells

Ginger

Energy- Masculine/ Yang
Elements- Fire
Planetary/ Deity Association- Mars/ Hecate
Magical Correspondents: Adds strength and speed

to spells, Defense, Healing, Hex breaking, Love, Power, Romance, Success
Magical Uses: Charm, Talisman, Tonic
Health Benefits: Anti-Inflammatory, relieves osteoarthritis, reduces appetite, relieves nausea and morning sickness

Witchy tip* Chew fresh ginger before spell work or rituals for added spiritual power

Grapes/ Raisins

Energy- Femine/ Neutral
Elements- Water
Planetary/ Deity Association- Moon/ Bacchus, Hathor, Het Heret, Iznagi
Magical Correspondences: Dream magic, Enhanced mental strength, Fertility, Garden magic, Love, Peace, Prosperity, Psychic awareness
Magical Uses: Powder, Talisman,
Health Benefits: Contains vitamins C and K, may regulate blood pressure and blood sugar levels
Witchy tip* Carry dried grape seeds in our wallet to attract money

Honey

Energy- Femine/ Yin
Elements- Water
Planetary/ Deity Associations- Sun/ Oshun, Ra, Demeter
Magical Correspondences: Beauty, Binding, Compelling, Happiness, Healing, Love, Lust, Wealth
Magical Uses: Spiritual bath, Candle dress, Jar spells

Health Benefits: Antifungal, antibacterial, antiviral, relieves symptoms of colds and flues, promotes healthy skin and hair

Witchy tip* write targets name on paper cover with honey, burn a candle over to sweeten the person's feelings towards you

Honeydew Melon

Energy- Femine
Elements- Water
Planetary/ Deity Associations- Oshun
Magical Correspondences: Beauty, Fertility, Prosperity, Immortality
Magical Uses: Amulets, Powders
Health Benefits: High in Copper, Fiber and vitamin C. Strengthens teeth and bones

Witchy tip* Ground the seeds of a honeydew melon into powder. Use in rituals/ spells for slow timing attractions (Future aspiration such as dream home, retlrement goal ect)

Lemon

Energy- Femenine/ Yin
Elements- Water, Fire
Planetary/ Deity Associations- Sun, Moon/ Oshun, Jambhala
Magical Correspondences: Cleansing, Friendship, Happiness, Longevity, Purification, Renewal, Romance, Spiritual energy boost, Stop gossip, Souring situations
Magical Uses: Inscensce, Powder, Spiritual bath

Health Benefits: Rich source of electrolytes, and vitamin C, treats colds and flu, improves digestion, promotes brain health

Marjoram

Energy- Masculine/ Yang
Elements- Air
Planetary/ Deity Associations- Mercury, Venus/ Aphrodite
Magical Correspondence: Courage, Dream work, Grieving, Happiness, Love, Money, Protection, Psychic development, Psychic protection, Spirit work
Magical Uses: Charm
Health benefits: Anti-Inflammatory, Antioxidant, prevents wrinkles, aide with depression, and digestion

Witchy tip* Add marjoram to your bath when healing from heartbreak or to the pain of ease mourning

Mint

Energy- Masculine/ Yang
Elements- Air
Planetary/ Deity Associations - Mercury, Pluto / Demeter, Hades, Hecate, Presephone
Magical Correspondences: Cleansing, Consecration, Exorcism, Focus, Happiness, Love, Lust, Money, Protection, Purification, Release, Renewal, Sleep spells, Success, Travel
Magical Uses: Charm
Health Benefits: Anti Inflammatory, Antibacterial,

relieves upset stomach, calms anxiety, improves memory

Witchy tip* Chew mint leaves before casting acts of love or lust for added vigor

Mustard Seeds

Energy- Masculine/ Yang
Elements- Water
Planetary/ Deity Associations- Sun, Mars
Magical Correspondents: Courage, Curses, Commanding, Enhances mental strength, Exorcism, Fertility, Good luck, Health, Passion, Spell breaking, Success
Magical Uses: Charm
Health Benefits: Anti Inflammatory, high in selenium, magnesium, and iron, reduces asthma related symptoms, lowers blood pressure and relieves arthritis

Lore* Said to be one of the oldest known good luck charms. Add mustard seeds to mojo bags or carry when in need of luck or good fortune

Nutmeg

Energy- Masculine/ Yang
Elements- Fire
Planetary/ Deity Associations- Jupiter/ Many of the Indian Gods and Goddess
Magical Correspondents: Fast money, Fertility, Legal matters, Luck, Prosperity, Spiritual strength, Success
Magical Uses: Charm, Talisman

Health Benefits: Anti Inflammatory, relieves arthritis pain, Aids digestion, sleep aid, boost brain function, improves skin health

Lore* Drill a whole into the nutmeg, fill with liquid mercury or quicksilver and seal with wax. Carry with you while gambing for prosperous outcomes.

Olives

Energy- Maculine/ Neutral
Elements- Fire
Planetary/ Deity Associations- Sun/ Aten, Aphrodite, Athena, Ra, Minerva, Apollo
Magical Correspondences: Dispel enemies, Fertility, Good luck, Healing, Lust, Meditation, Peace, Protection, Raising vibration, Releasing negativity, Sexual potency
Magical Uses: Talisman, Oil
Health Benefits: Powerful antioxidant, high in vitamin E, Promotes healthy skin, hair and bones

Witchy tip* Place three olive pits under your bedding to raise sexual energy

Onion

Energy- Masculine/ Yang
Elements- Fire
Planetary/ Deity Associations- Moon, Mars, Jupiter/ Isis
Magical Correspondences: Contacting other realms, Endurance, Exorcism, Healing, Lunar rights and rituals, Lust, Prophetic dreams, Prosperity, Protection, Stability,
Magical Uses: Charm, Talisman

Health Benefits: High in dietary fibers, magnesium and antioxidants, reduces scarring, aides in heart health, lowers cholesterol

Lore* Burn the shell of an onion peel white/ yellow to protect the home, red to insight passion between two people

Oranges

Energy- Female/ Yang
Elements- Fire
Planetary/ Deity Association- Venus/ Enlil
Magical Correspondences: Divination, Emotional balance, Happiness, Luck, Love, Money, Peace, Stability
Magical Uses: Incense, Talisman
Health Benefits: High in vitamin C and antioxidants, kights viral infections, promotes kidney health, good for healthy teeth and bones

Witchy Tip* Burn dried orange peels during money rituals for added power

Oregano

Energy- Masculin
Elements- Air
Planetary/ Deity Association- Venus
Magical Correspondences: Dream work, Love, Luck, Removal, Protecton
Magical Uses: Amulet, Bath, Incense, Potion
Health Benefits: High in Vitamin K, Soothes upset stomach and sea sickness, Eases symptoms of bronchitis and colds.

Witchy Tip* Burn oregano to cleanse the home of unwanted energy

Peaches

Energy- Female/ Yin
Elements- Water
Planetary/Deity Associations- Venus, Hai Wang Ma, Iznagi
Magical Correspondences: Exorcism, Fertility, Longevity, Love, Protection, Wishes, Wisdom
Magical Uses: Incense, Powder, Talisman
Health Benefits: Contains vitamins C, A and E Aids in digestion, good for skin and eye health

Lore* Due to its believed ability to grant wishes, peach tree wood is commonly used to construct wands and other magical tools for conjure

Rice

Energy- Female/ Yin
Elements- Earth
Planetary/ Deity Associations- Sun/ All mother deities
Magical Correspondences: Abundance, Blessings, Fertility, Grounding, Protection, Rain magic, Security, Wealth, Working with spirits
Magical Uses: Talisman
Health Benefits: High in fiber, Improves digestive health

Witchy tip* Use rice to ground candles in spell work for prosperity

Rosemary

Energy- Masculine/ Yan
Elements-Fire
Planetary/ Deity Associations- Sun, Pluto/ Mary
Magical Correspondences: Blessings, Consecrating, Dream work, Evoktion, Elves, Exorcism, Good luck, Grieving, Happiness, Healing, Love, Lust, Mental strength, Passion, Psychic protection and development, Purification, Youth
Magical Uses: Inscensce, Charm
Health Benefits: Relieves muscle spasms, reduces inflammation, Improves mood and memory, supports circulatory health.

Witchy tip* Rosemary can be used safely as a substitute for any herb in any spell work or ritual practice

Saffron

Energy- Masculine/ Yang
Elements- Fire
Planetary/ Deity Association- Sun/ Ra, Eos, Brahma
Magical Correspondences: Clairvoyance, Commanding, Divination, Happiness, Healing, Joy, Leadership, Love, Lust, Prosperity, Psychic enhancer, Spell breaking, Strength, Weather spells (Wind),
Magical Uses: Charm, Inscensce, Potion
Health Benefits: Antioxidant, aphrodisiac, relieves symptoms of PMS, improves moods, speeds healing time of wounds

Witchy tip* Add saffron to wine/ drink, serve to the one you desire for lusting effects

Sage
Energy- Masculine/ Yang
Elements- Air
Planetary/ Deity Associations- Sun, Mercury, Jupiter, Earth
Magical Correspondences:Cleansing, Domestic peace, Happiness, Healing, Immortality, Inspiration, Knowledge, Longevity, Money, Psychic development and protection, Protection, Reversal magic, Secrets, Success, Wisdom, Wishes
Magical Uses: Inscensce, Bath, Candle dress
Health Benefits: Increase memory, relieves sore throat pain, helps lower cholesterol, relieves symptoms of diarrhea

Witchy tip* Add sage to floor was to remove negative energy from home or any space

Sea Salt
Energy- Femine/ Yang
Elements- Earth
Planetary/ Deity Associations- Earth/ Yemaya
Magical Correspondences:Banishment, Blessings, Cleansing, Exorcism, Healing, Protection, Removal of curses,
Magical Uses: Bath, Talisman
Health Benefits: Helps maintain healthy electrolyte balance, natural treatment for psoriasis

Witchy tip* Add salt to bath water to cleanse
negative and unwanted energy

Strawberry
Energy- Femine/ Yin
Elements- Water
Planetary/ Deity Associations- Venus/ Freya
Magical Correspondences: Favorable outcomes,
Love, Luck, Passion, Success
Magical Uses: Talisman, Inscensce
Health Benefits: Good source of vitamin C,
promotes healthy teeth and hair, improves brain
health

Lore* Place strawberry leaves in a dish inside of
the home to usher in good luck

Tabasco Sauce
Energy- Masculine/ Yang
Elements- Fire
Planetary/ Deity Association- Mars
Magical Correspondences: Empowerment,
Heartbreak, Hexing, Increase aura,
Overcome heartbreak, Protection, Romance,
Separation, Speeds spells
Magical Uses: Talisman
Health Benefits: Antioxidant, anti inflammatory, aids
digestion, relieves migraine pain

Witchy tip* add tabasco sauce to your candle
dressing to increase power and speed up spells

Tarragon

Energy- Femine/ Yin
Elements- Fire
Planetary/ Deity Associations- Sun, Mars/ Artemis
Magical Correspondences:Cause pain, Commanding, Compassion, Courage, Dragons, End abusive relationships, Good luck, Keeping secrets, Love, Peace, Protection, Strength
Magical Uses: Inscensce, Charm, Candle dress
Health Benefits: Contains magnesium, potassium and iron. Helps regulate sleep, reduces nausea, helps reduce blood sugar

Witchy tip* Burn tarragon to invoke the courage to end an abusive relationship/ habits

Thyme

Energy- Femine/ Yin
Elements- Water
Planetary/ Deity Associations- Sun, Venus
Magical Correspondences: Beauty, Contacting other realms, Courage, Dreams, Fairies, Fidelity, Grieving, Happiness, Healing, Love, Prosperity, Psychic and divination work,
Purification
Magical Uses: Inscensce, Charm, Candle dress
Health Benefits:Antifungal, antioxidant properties. Treats respiratory issues, bug bites and stings.

Witchy tip* Add thyme to prosperity baths to keep money flowing

Turmeric

Energy- Masculine/ Yang
Elements- Fire
Planetary/ Deity Associations- Mars
Magical Correspondences: Banishing, Beauty, Commanding, Confidence, Exorcism, Healing, Passion, Purification, Spell breaking, Strength
Magical Uses:Candle dress, Bath
Health Benefits: Anti inflammatory, antioxidant, antibacterial properties, relieves arthritis related pain, whiteness teeth, Improves memory, improves skin appearance

Witchy tip* Add tumeric to baths to promote self love and physical beauty

Vanilla

Energy- Femine/ Yin
Elements- Water
Planetary/ Deity Associations- Venus
Magical Correspondences: Beauty, Compassion, Fidelity, Forgiveness, Happiness, Joy, Love, Luck, Lust, Meditation, Reconciliation,Youth
Magical Uses: Inscencs, Powder, Talisman
Health Benefits: Natural antidepressant, improves digestion and dental health, relieves nausea

Witchy tip* Add crushed vanilla bean to your love/ lust spells for added energy

Vinegar

Energy- Masculine/ Yang
Elements- Fire

Planetary/ Deity Associations- Mars
Magical Correspondences: Banishing, Cleansing,
Hexing, Protection,
Magical Uses: Bath, Floor wash
Health Benefits: Fat free and nutrient rich, aids in
digestion, relieves skill ailments such as sunburn,
insect and jellyfish stings

Witchy Tip* Wash floors and windows with vinegar
to prevent evil spirits from entering

Watermelon

Energy- Femine/ Yin
Elements- Water
Planetary/ Deity Associations- Moon, Set, Yemaya
Magical Correspondences: Fertility, Healing,
Peace, Removing blockages, Vitality
Magical Uses: Amulet, Bath, Potion
Health Benefits: Hydrating, sexual stimulant, used
to treat abrasions of the skin and tired eyes.

Witchy Tip* After the death of a loved one, roll a
watermelon across your threshold and out the door
to assist in safe passage to the afterlife.

Check out my Etsy shop
www.magicalbeginningshop.com
For energy enhancing, spiritual cleansing bath
blends teas and products

Follow Magical Beginnings on social media to stay
up to date on new releases, products, services and
everyday magic tips and trick

Facebook @magicalbeginnings
Instagram @magicalbeginnings35
Twitter   @magicalbeginni1

Check out my Everyday Magic blog
Magicalbeginningshop.blogspot.com

Email me at
Believe@magicalbeginningshop.com

www.ingramcontent.com/pod-product-compliance
Lightning Source LLC
Chambersburg PA
CBHW051425250726
48655CB00003B/1240